This book belongs to:

_____

khob khun
 Thai

© Copyright 2021-2025 - All rights reserved.

You may not reproduce, duplicate or send the contents of this book without direct written permission from the author. You cannot hereby despite any circumstance blame the publisher or hold him or her to legal responsibility for any reparation, compensations, or monetary forfeiture owing to the information included herein, either in a direct or an indirect way.

Legal Notice: This book has copyright protection. You can use the book for personal purpose. You should not sell, use, alter, distribute, quote, take excerpts or paraphrase in part or whole the material contained in this book without obtaining the permission of the author first.

Disclaimer Notice: You must take note that the information in this document is for casual reading and entertainment purposes only. We have made every attempt to provide accurate, up to date and reliable information. We do not express or imply guarantees of any kind. The persons who read admit that the writer is not occupied in giving legal, financial, medical or other advice. We put this book content by sourcing various places.

Please consult a licensed professional before you try any techniques shown in this book. By going through this document, the book lover comes to an agreement that under no situation is the author accountable for any forfeiture, direct or indirect, which they may incur because of the use of material contained in this document, including, but not limited to, —errors, omissions, or inaccuracies.

 # KOR KAI
(Chicken)

ข KHOR KHAI
(Egg)

 # KHOR KHUAD
(Bottle)

 # KOR KHWAI
(Buffalo)

 # KOR KON
(Person)

 # KOR RAKANG
(Bell)

 # NGOR NGOO
(Snake)

 # JOR JARN
(Dish)

 # CHOR CHING
(Small Cymbal)
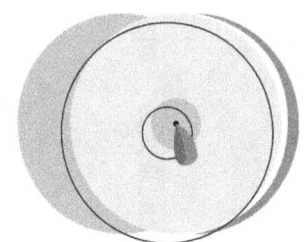

ช CHOR CHANG
(Elephant)

 # SOR SOE
(Chain)

 CHOR CHER
(Tree)

 # YOR YING
(Woman)

 # TOR PATAG
(Spear)

 # DOR CHADAR
(Headdress)

 # THOR THARN
(Pedestal)

 # TOR POOTAO
(Old Man)

 # NOR NEAN
(Young Monk)

 # DOR DEAG
(Child)

TOR TAO
(Turtle)

 # THOR THUNG
(Bag)

ท TOR TAHARN
(Soldier)

ธ TOR TONG (Flag)

ณ NOR NHOO
(Mouse)

บ BOR BAIMAI
(Leaf)

ปู POR PLAR
(Fish)

 # POR PEUNG
(Bee)

 # PHOR PHAR
(Lid)
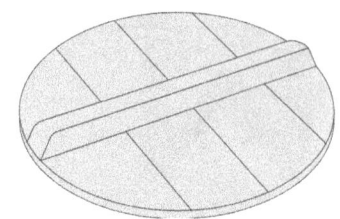

ฝ POR PARN
(Tray)

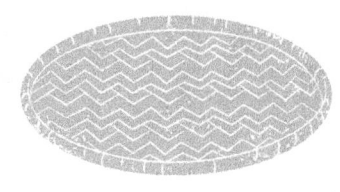

ฟัน FOR FUN
(Teeth)

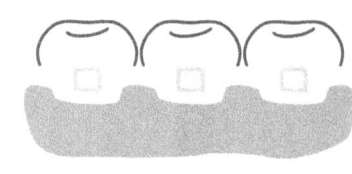

 # POR SUMPAO
(Junk)

ચ MOR MAR
(Horse)

ย YOR YAG
(Giant)

 ROR ROER
(Boat)

ล

LOR LING

(Monkey)

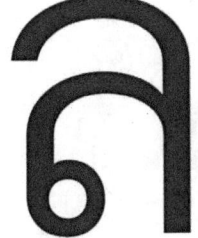

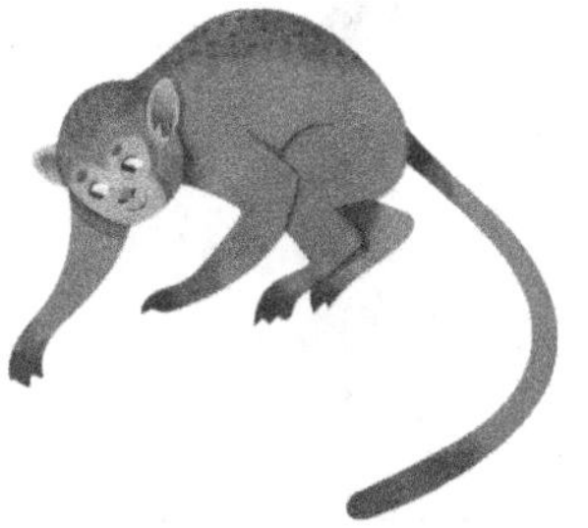

ล ล ล ล ล ล ล ล ล

ล ล ล ล ล ล ล ล ล

ล ล ล ล ล ล ล ล ล

ล ล ล ล ล ล ล ล ล

ㅇ WOR WHAEN
(Ring)

 # SOR SARLAR
(Pavilion)

 SOR REUSEE
(Ascetic)

ส SOR SOER

(Tiger)

ส ส ส ส ส ส ส ส

ส ส ส ส ส ส ส ส

ส ส ส ส ส ส ส ส

ส ส ส ส ส ส ส ส

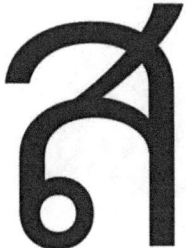

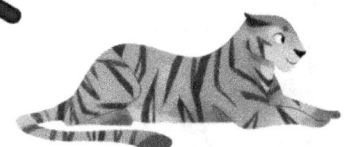

๚๘ HOR HEEB
(A Kind of Box)

LOR JULAR
(Kite)

 # OR ARNG
(Basin)
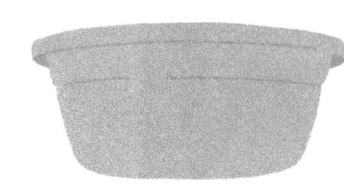

 # HOR NOGHOOG
(Owl)

−า AR อา

ดุ บ อุ

โ-ะ   OE   โอะ

โ- o โอ

เ◌ื eu อื

เ ยนน ดื่

ເ−ິ EA ເອິ

ເອິ ເອິ ເອິ ເອິ

ເອິ ເອິ ເອິ ເອິ

ເອິ ເອິ ເອິ ເອິ

ເອິ ເອິ ເອິ ເອິ

ແ-ະ AE ແອະ

แ- AIR แอ

เ-าะ OR เอาะ

เอาะ เอาะ เอาะ

เอาะ เอาะ เอาะ

เอาะ เอาะ เอาะ

เอาะ เอาะ เอาะ

ඏ Aw ඐ ඐ

ඐ ඐ ඐ ඐ ඐ ඐ ඐ ඐ

ඐ ඐ ඐ ඐ ඐ ඐ ඐ ඐ

ඐ ඐ ඐ ඐ ඐ ඐ ඐ ඐ

ඐ ඐ ඐ ඐ ඐ ඐ ඐ ඐ

เ-อะ ER เออะ

เ-อ EER เออ

เ-ียะ IA เอียะ

เ-ย EAR เอีย

เ-ือะ OER เอือะ

เอือะ เอือะ เอือะ

เอือะ เอือะ เอือะ

เอือะ เอือะ เอือะ

เอือะ เอือะ เอือะ

เ-ือ OEER เอือ

เอือ เอือ เอือ เอือ

เอือ เอือ เอือ เอือ

เอือ เอือ เอือ เอือ

เอือ เอือ เอือ เอือ

ັວະ UA ອັວະ

◌ัว   UAA   อัว

ອັວ ອັວ ອັວ ອັວ ອັວ

ອັວ ອັວ ອັວ ອັວ ອັວ

ອັວ ອັວ ອັວ ອັວ ອັວ

ອັວ ອັວ ອັວ ອັວ ອັວ

ำ ॥ำ อำ

อำ อำ อำ อำ อำ

อำ อำ อำ อำ อำ

อำ อำ อำ อำ อำ

อำ อำ อำ อำ อำ

ไ-   AI   ใอ

เ-า   AO   เอา

เอา เอา เอา เอา

เอา เอา เอา เอา

เอา เอา เอา เอา

เอา เอา เอา เอา

ୠ RE

ฤๅ   REH

ก LE

ภา   LEH

Please leave a review!

ขอขอบคุณ

khob khun

 Thai

www.ingramcontent.com/pod-product-compliance
Lightning Source LLC
LaVergne TN
LVHW081544060526
838200LV00048B/2210